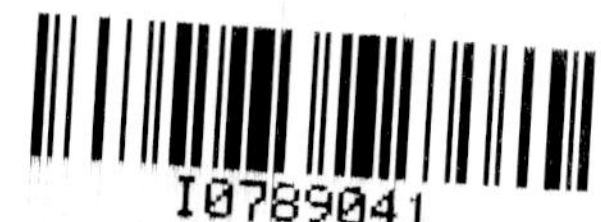

THIS BOOK

BELONG TO

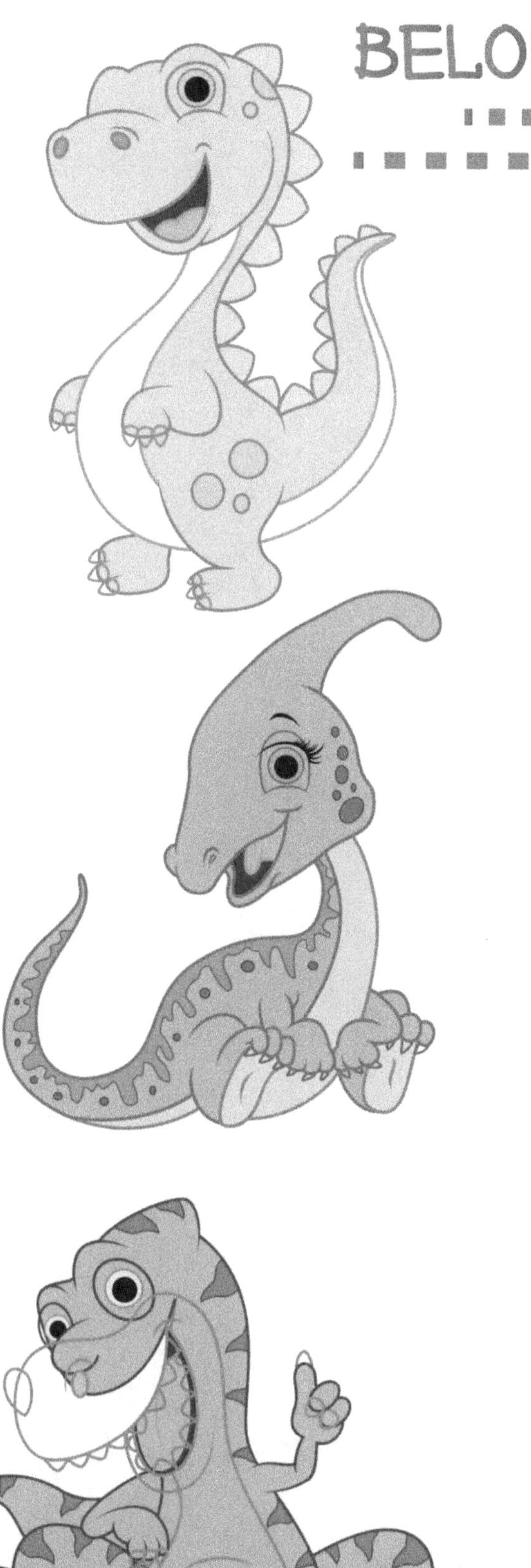
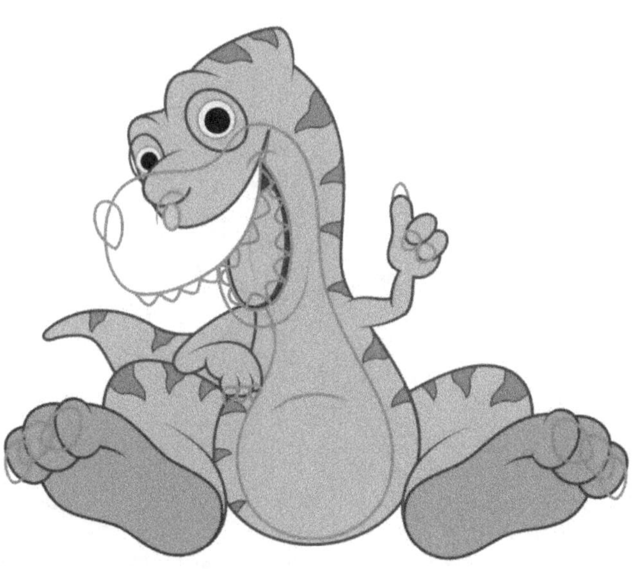
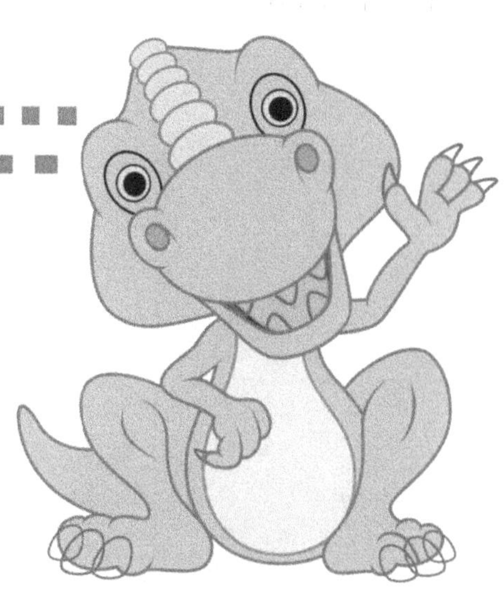
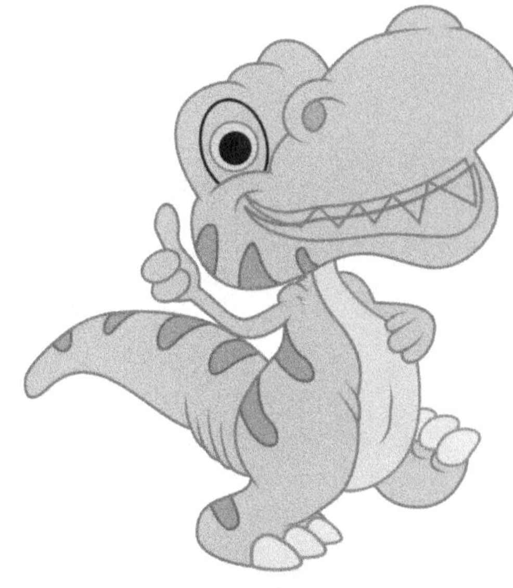
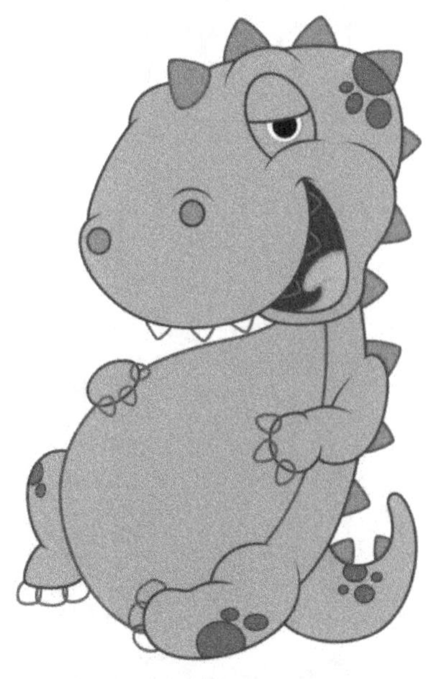

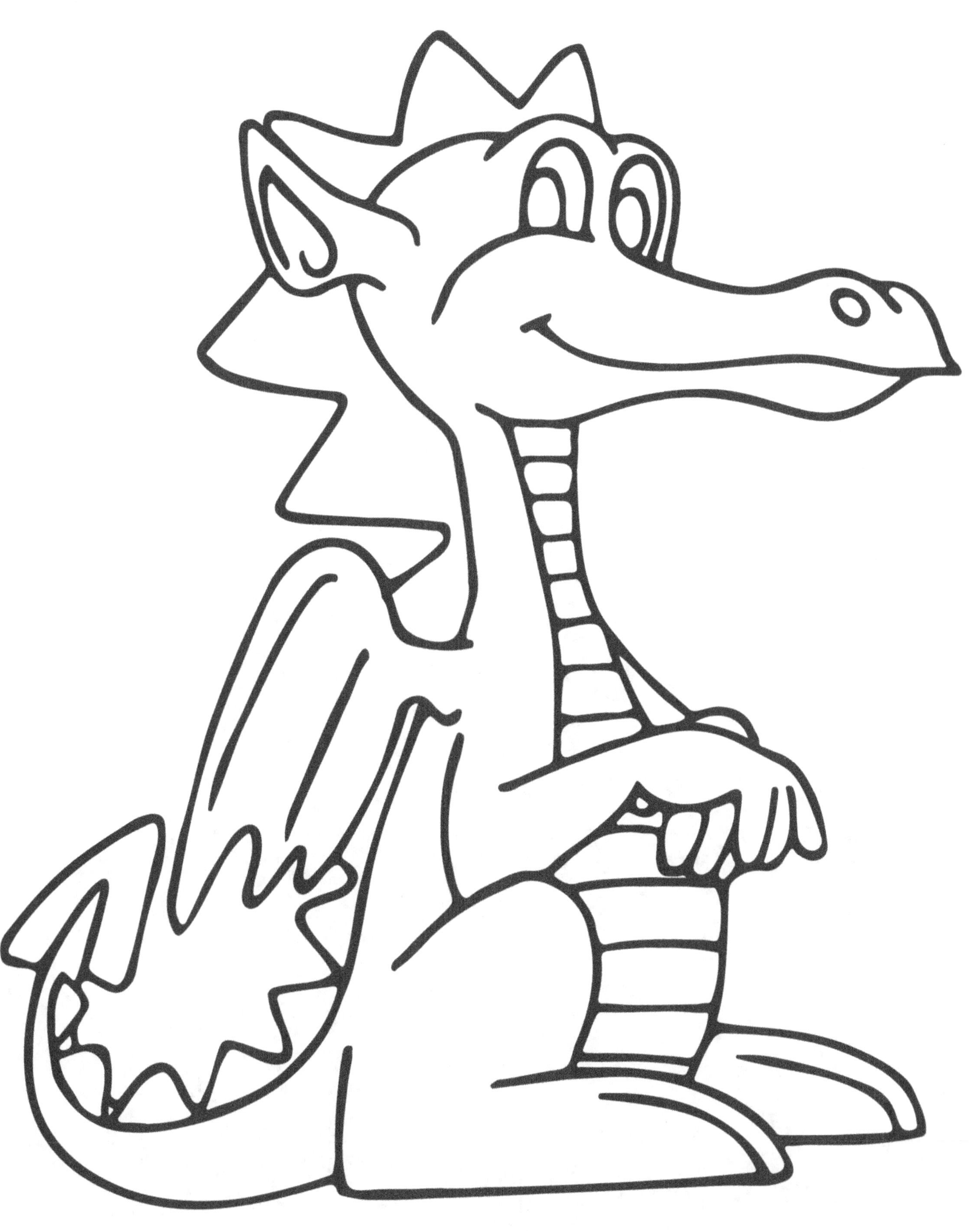

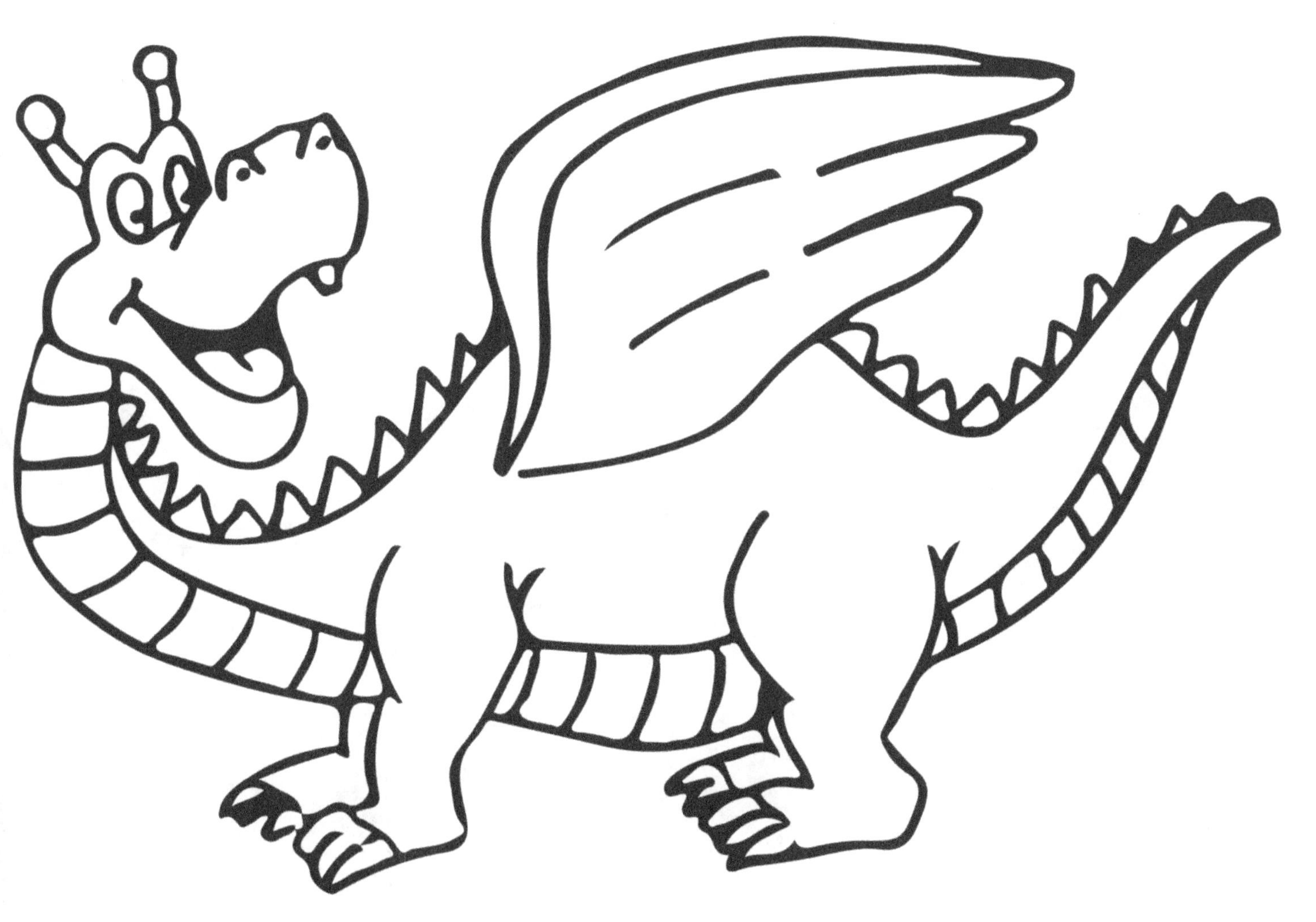

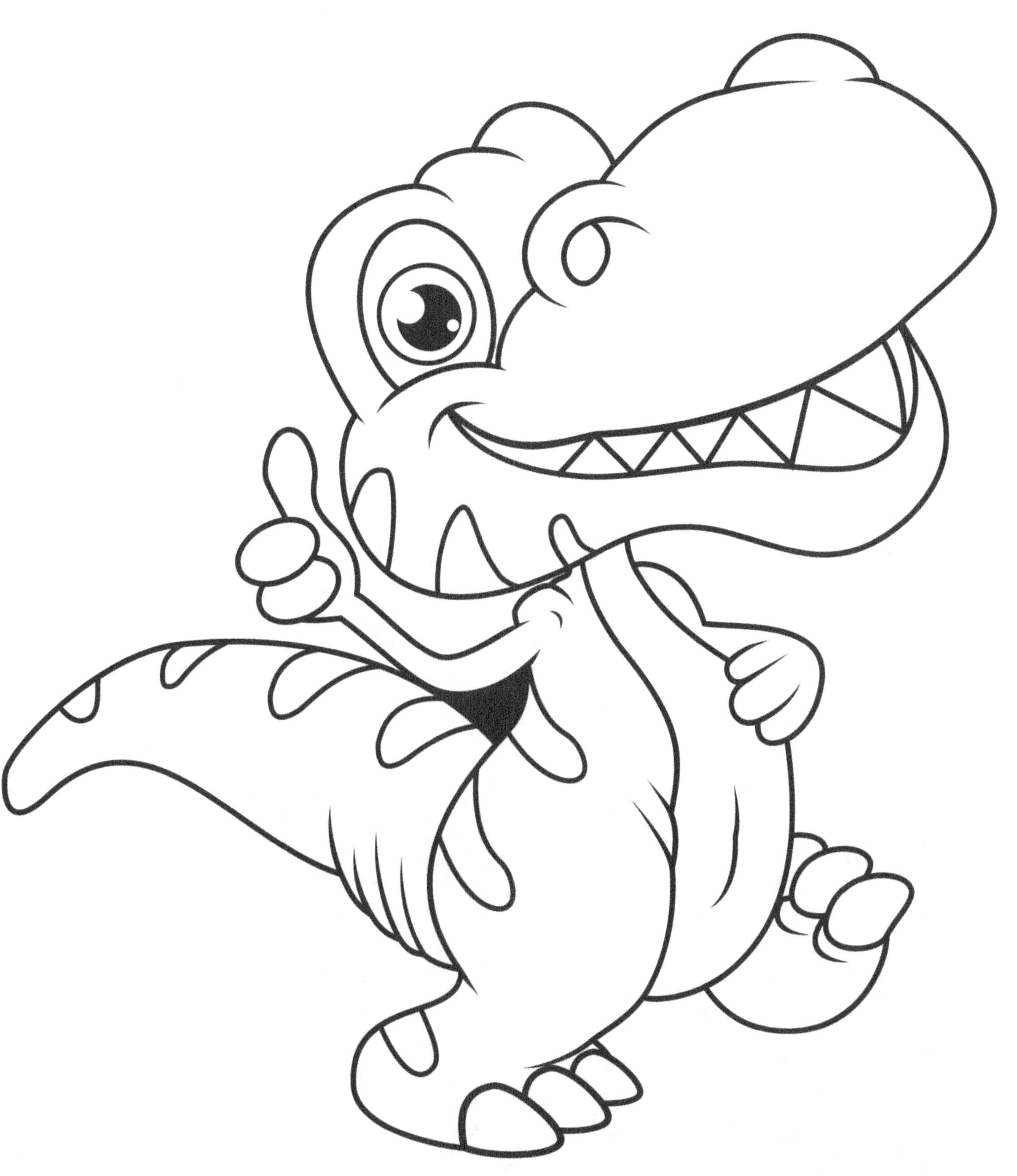

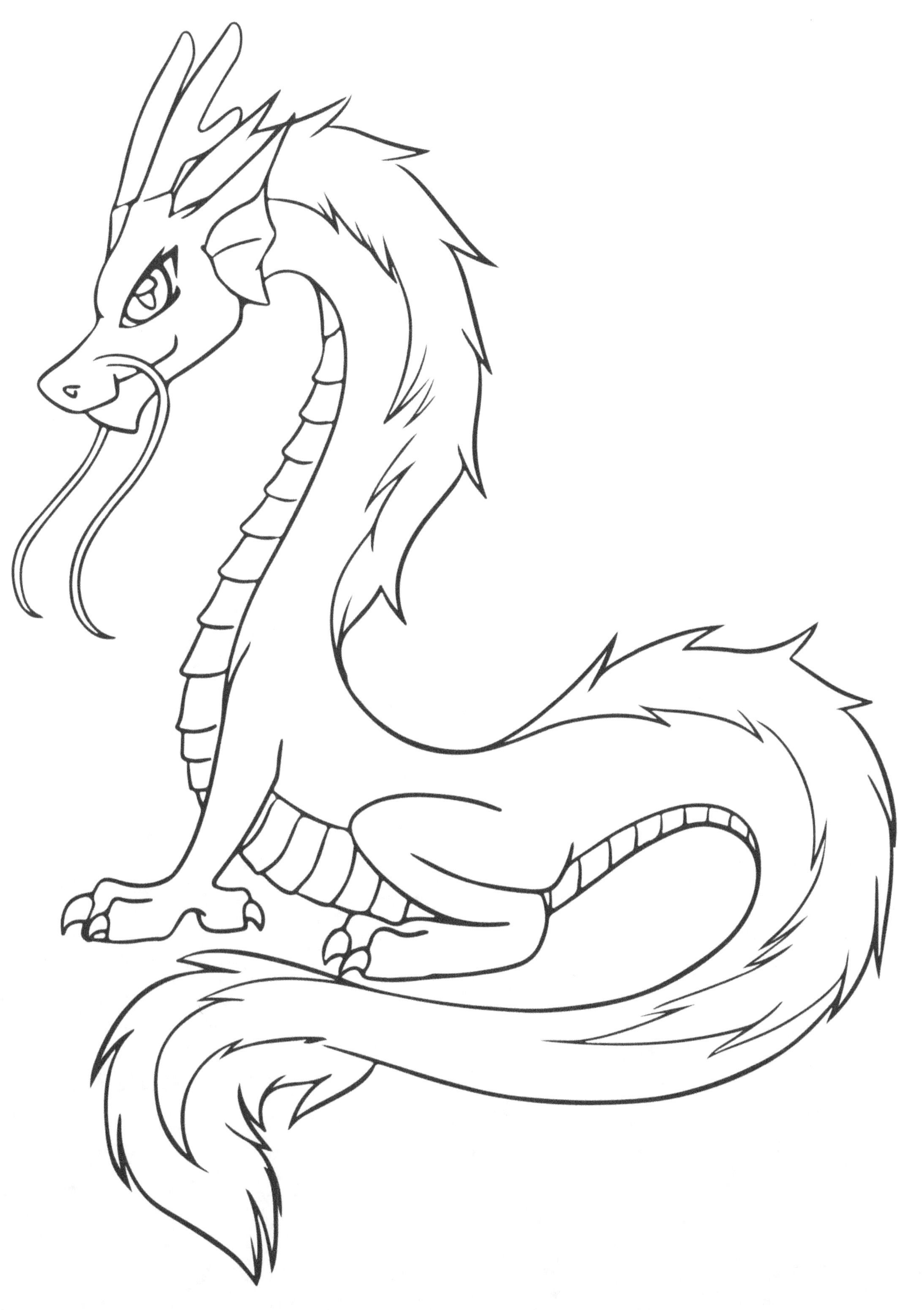

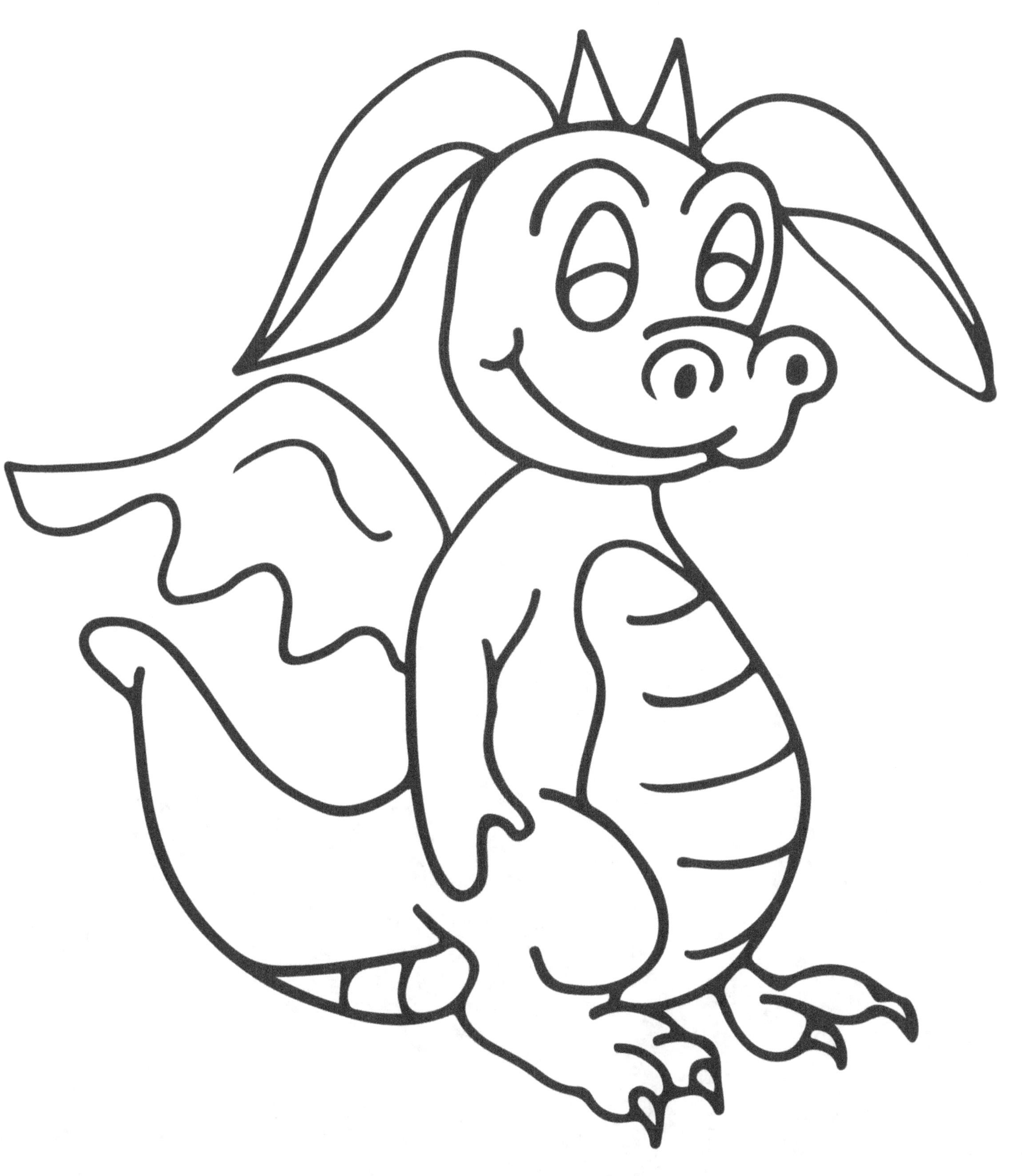

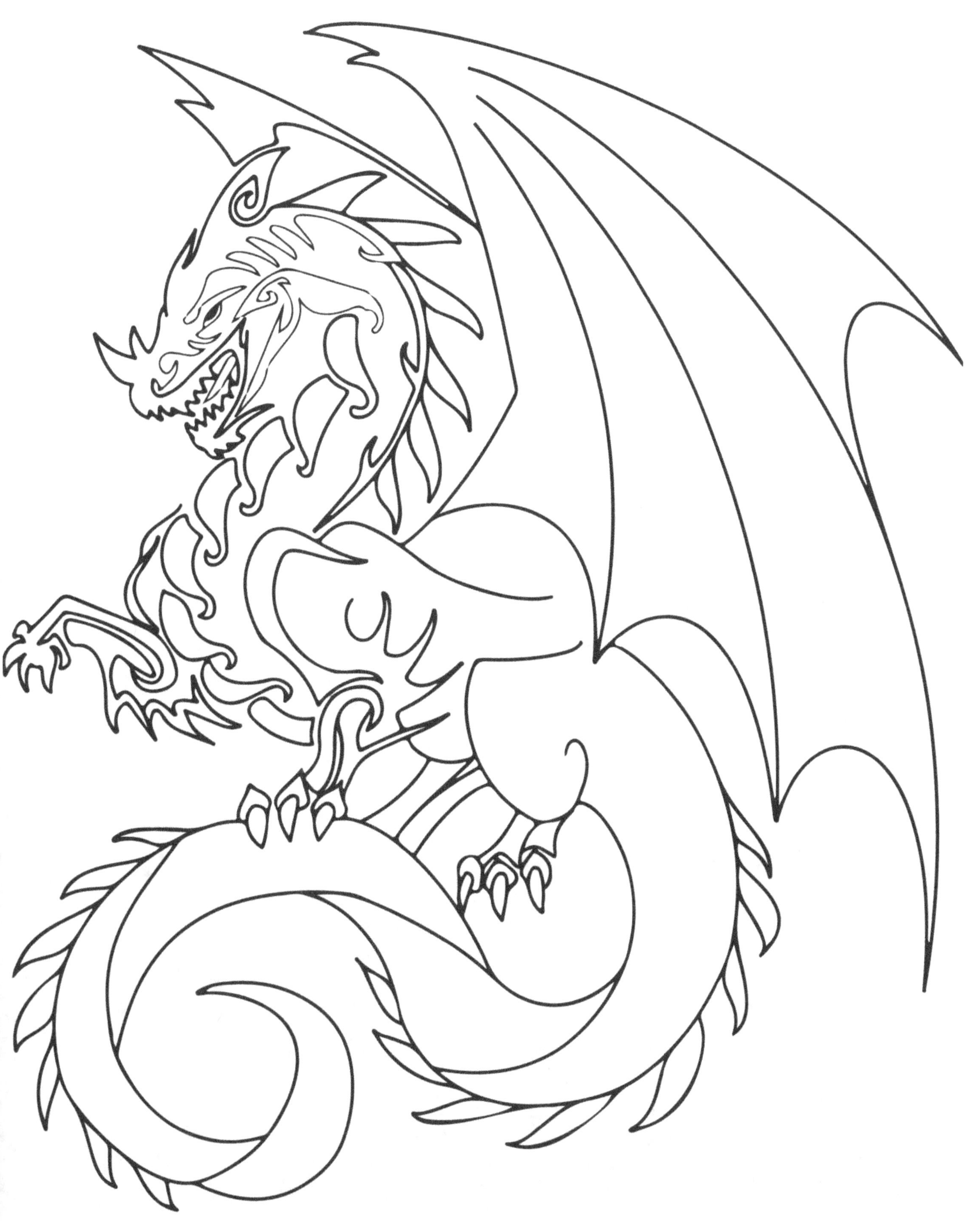

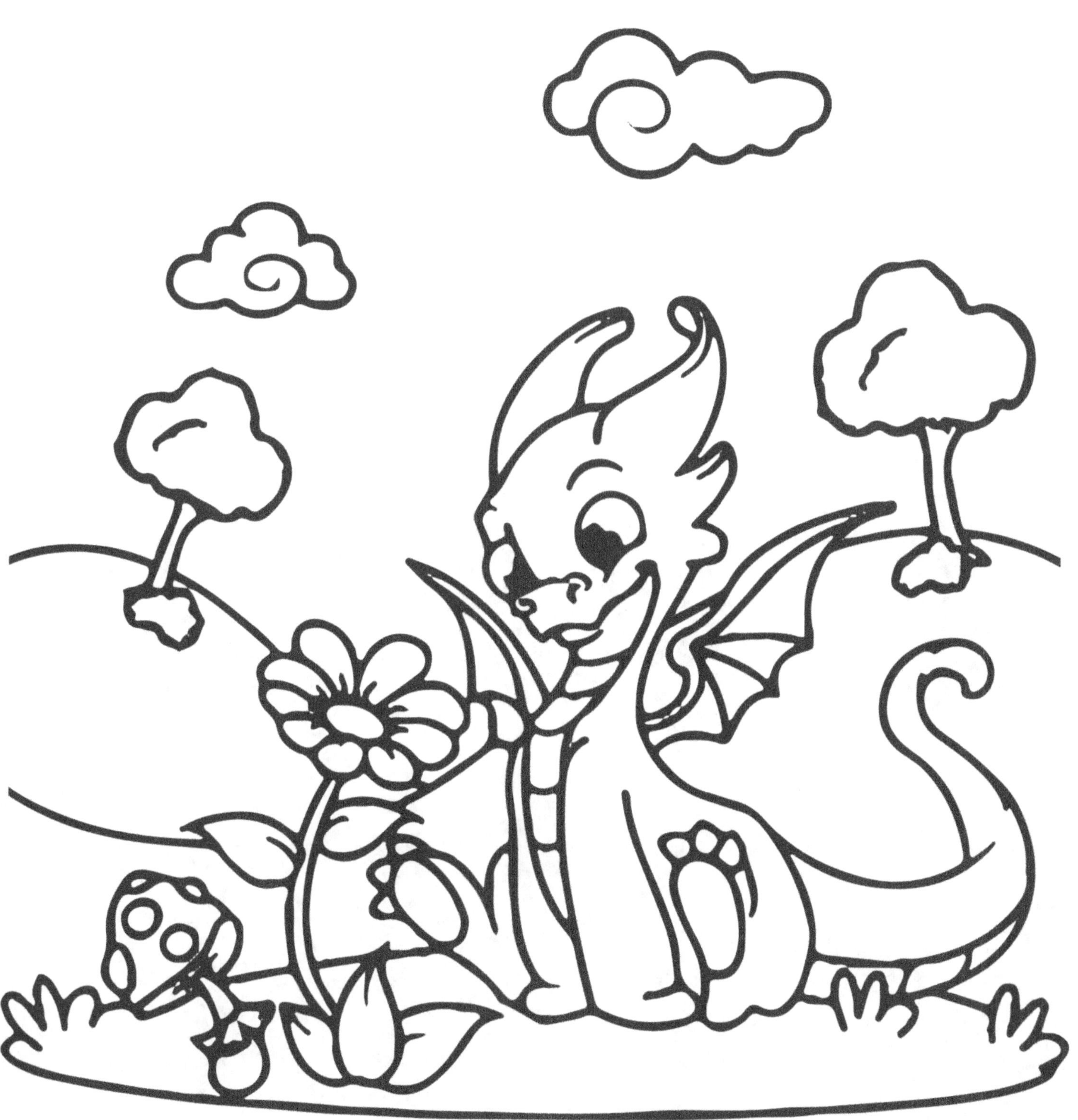

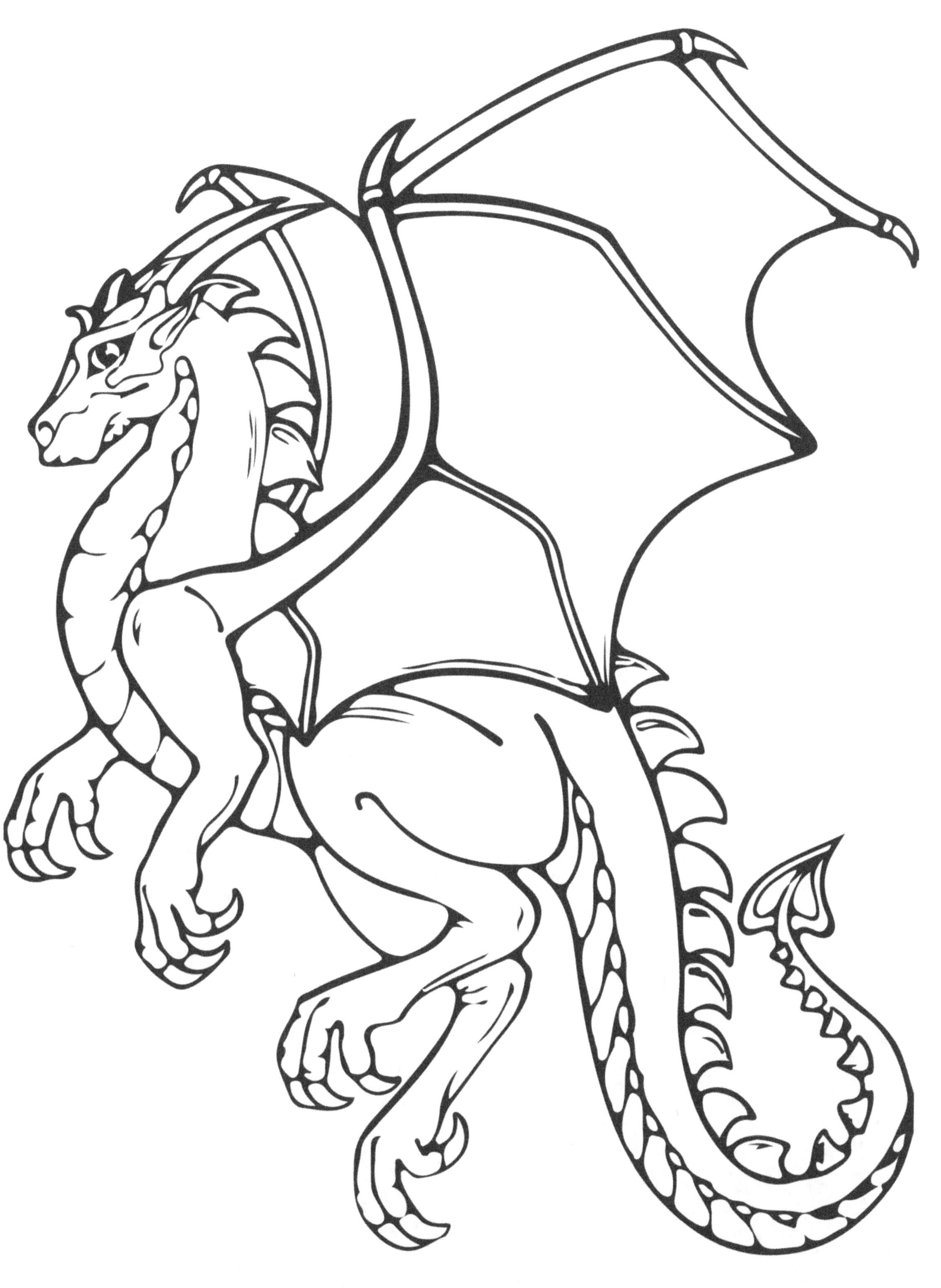

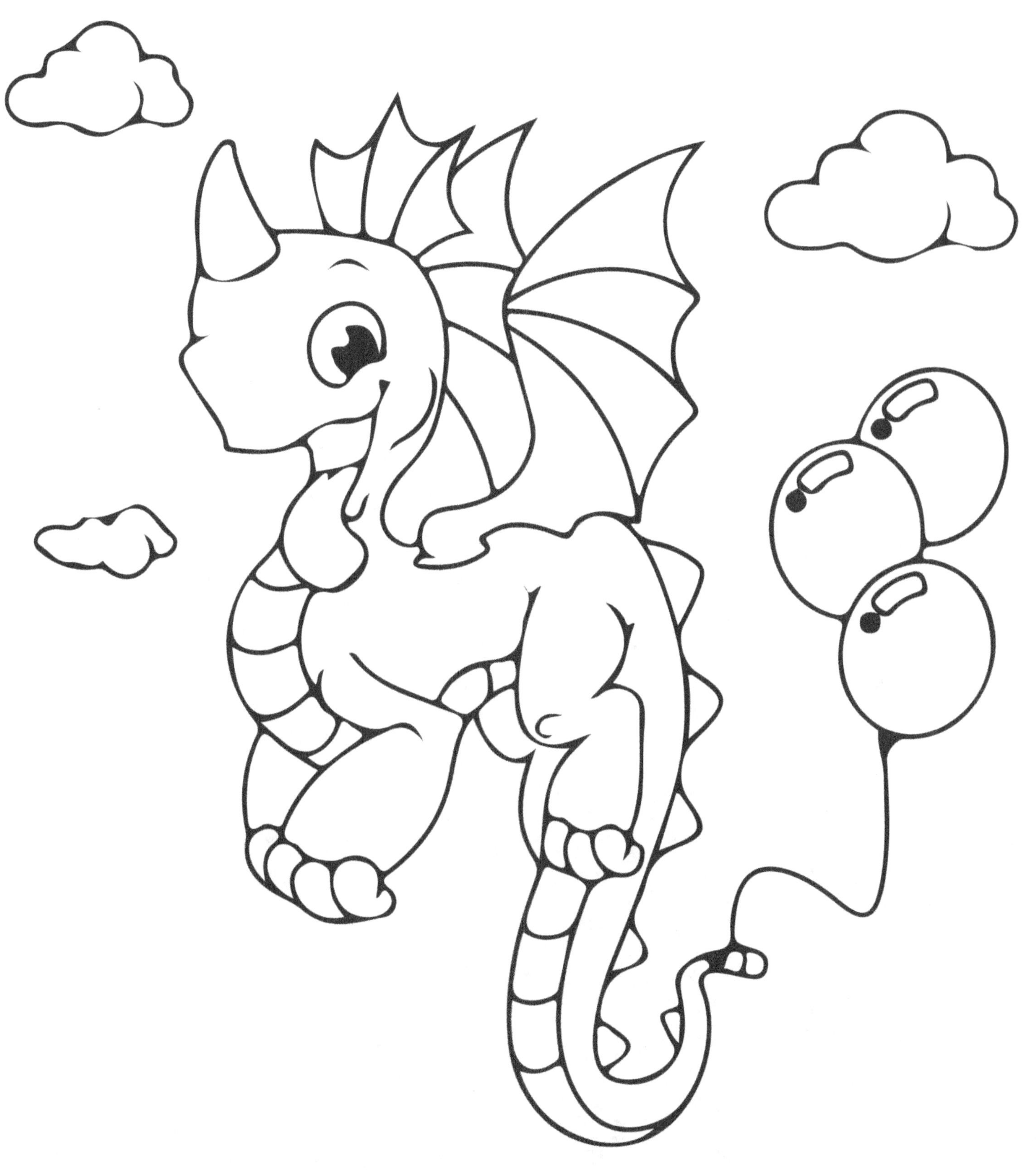

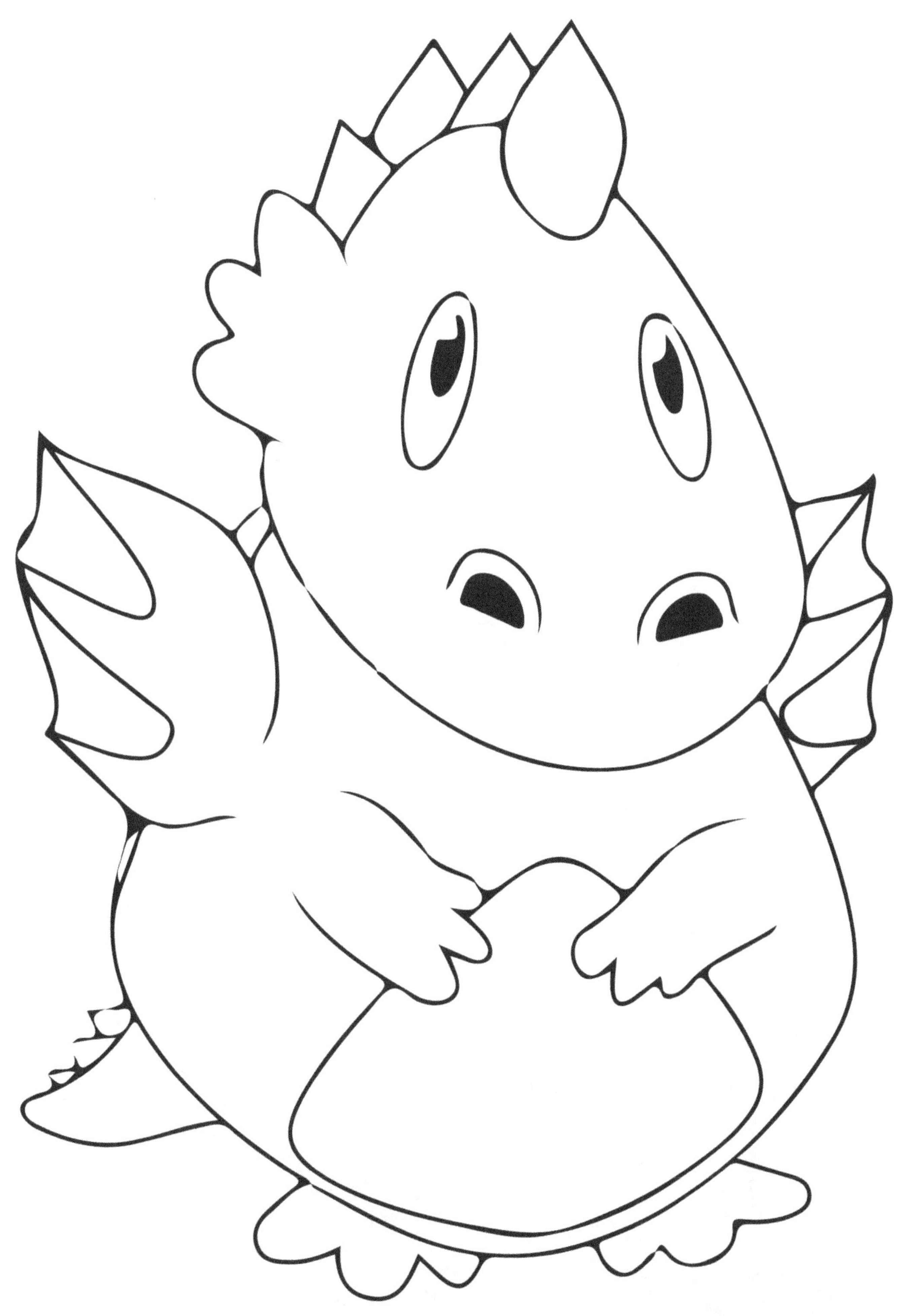

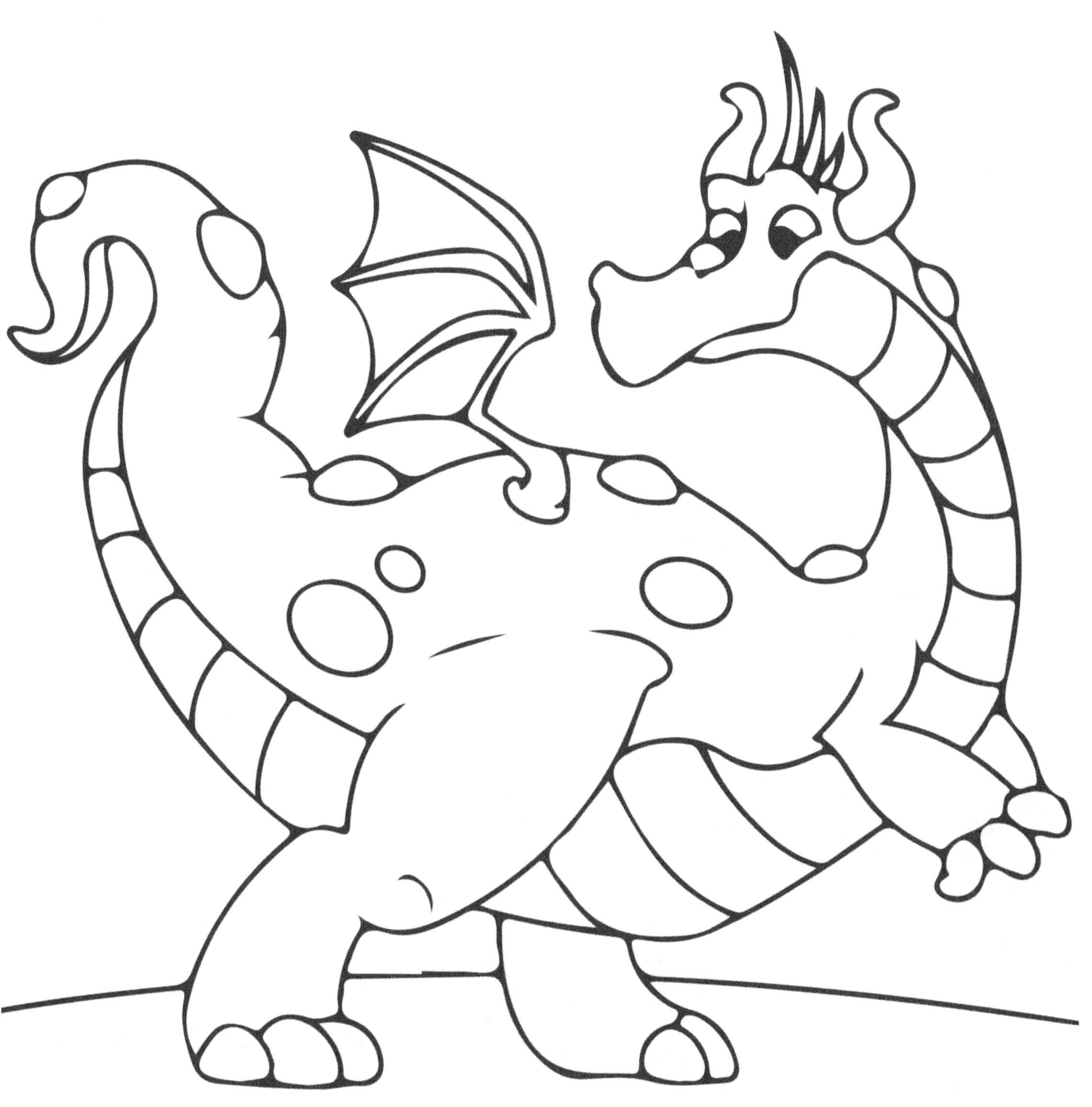

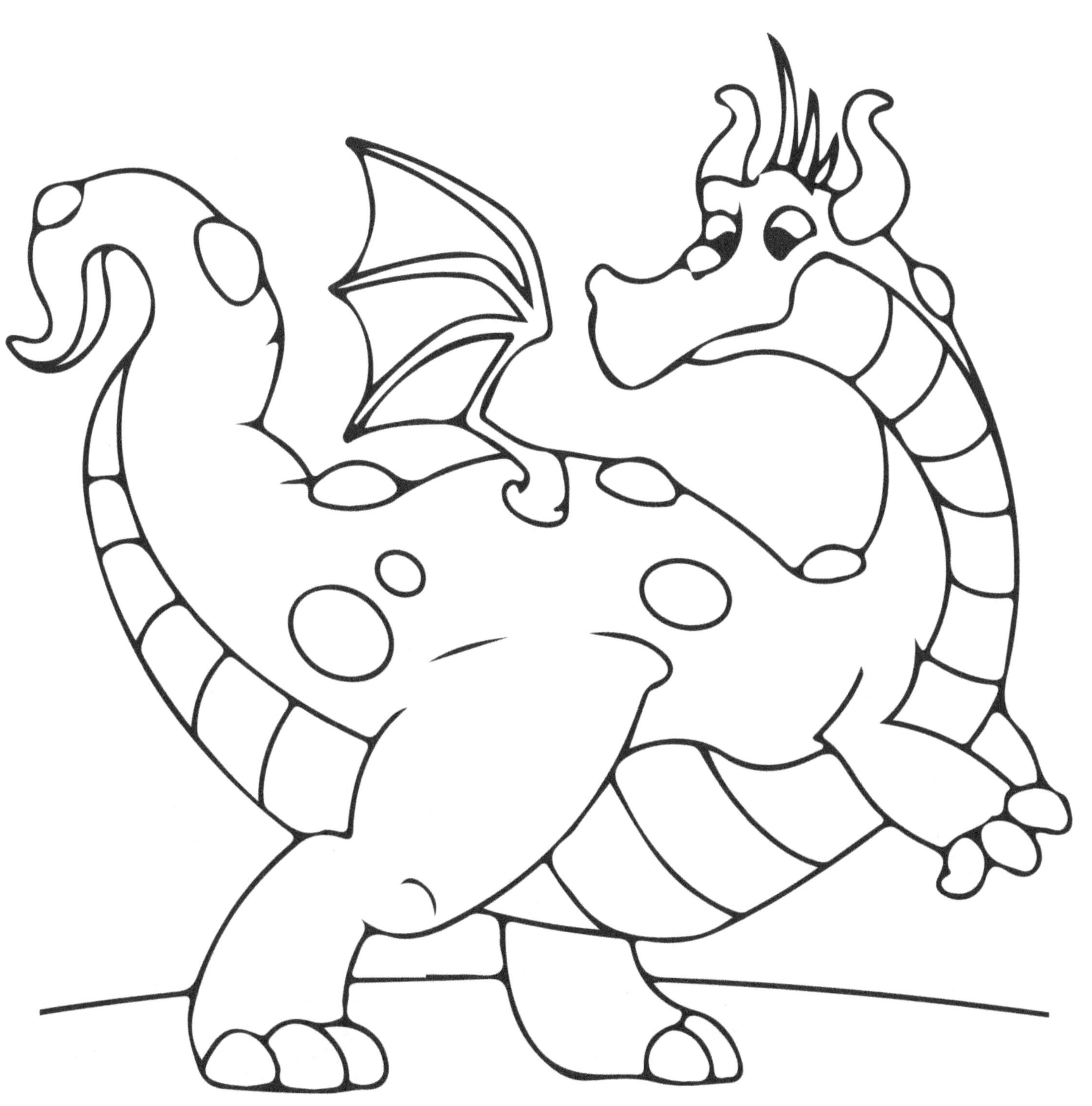

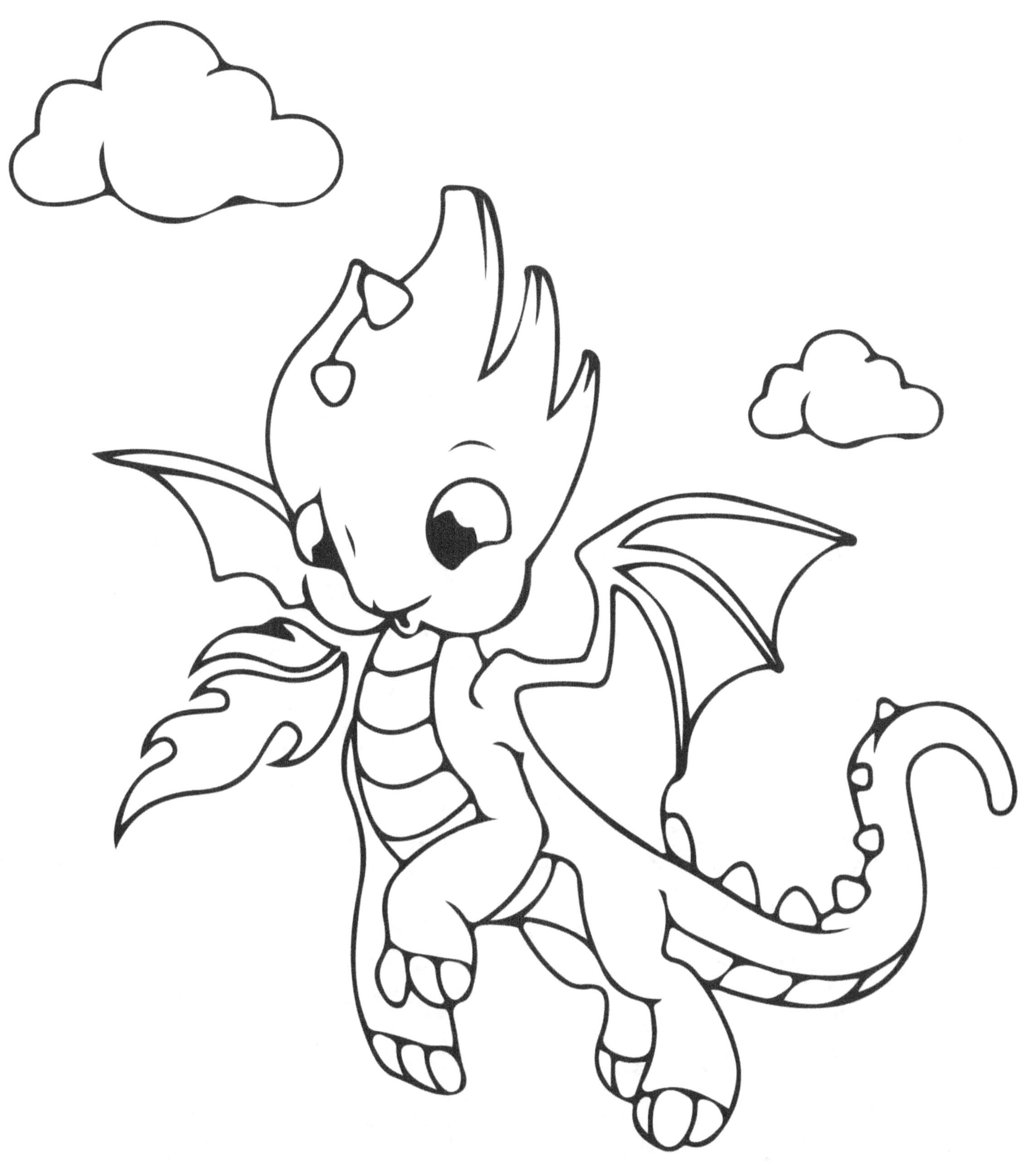

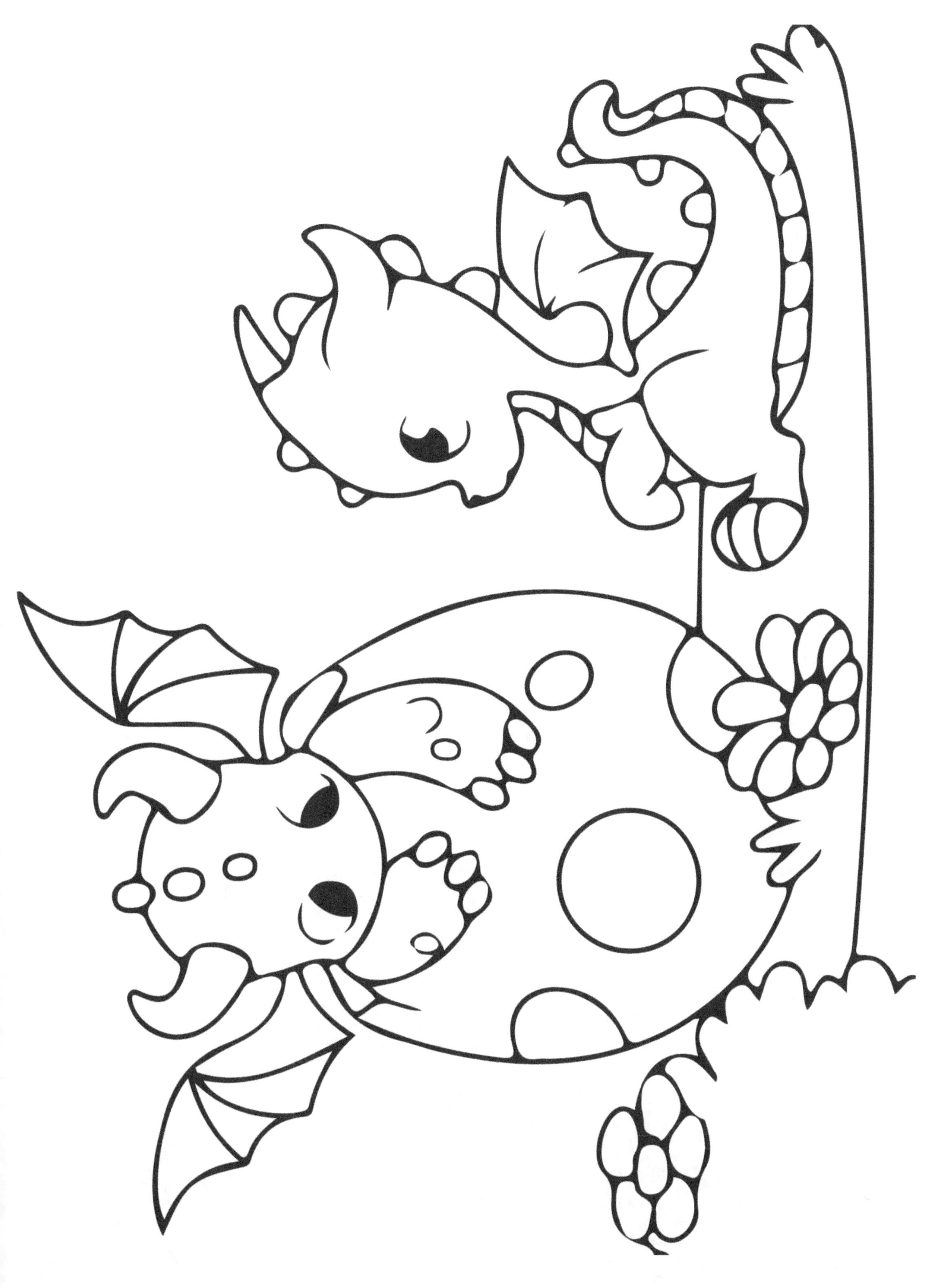

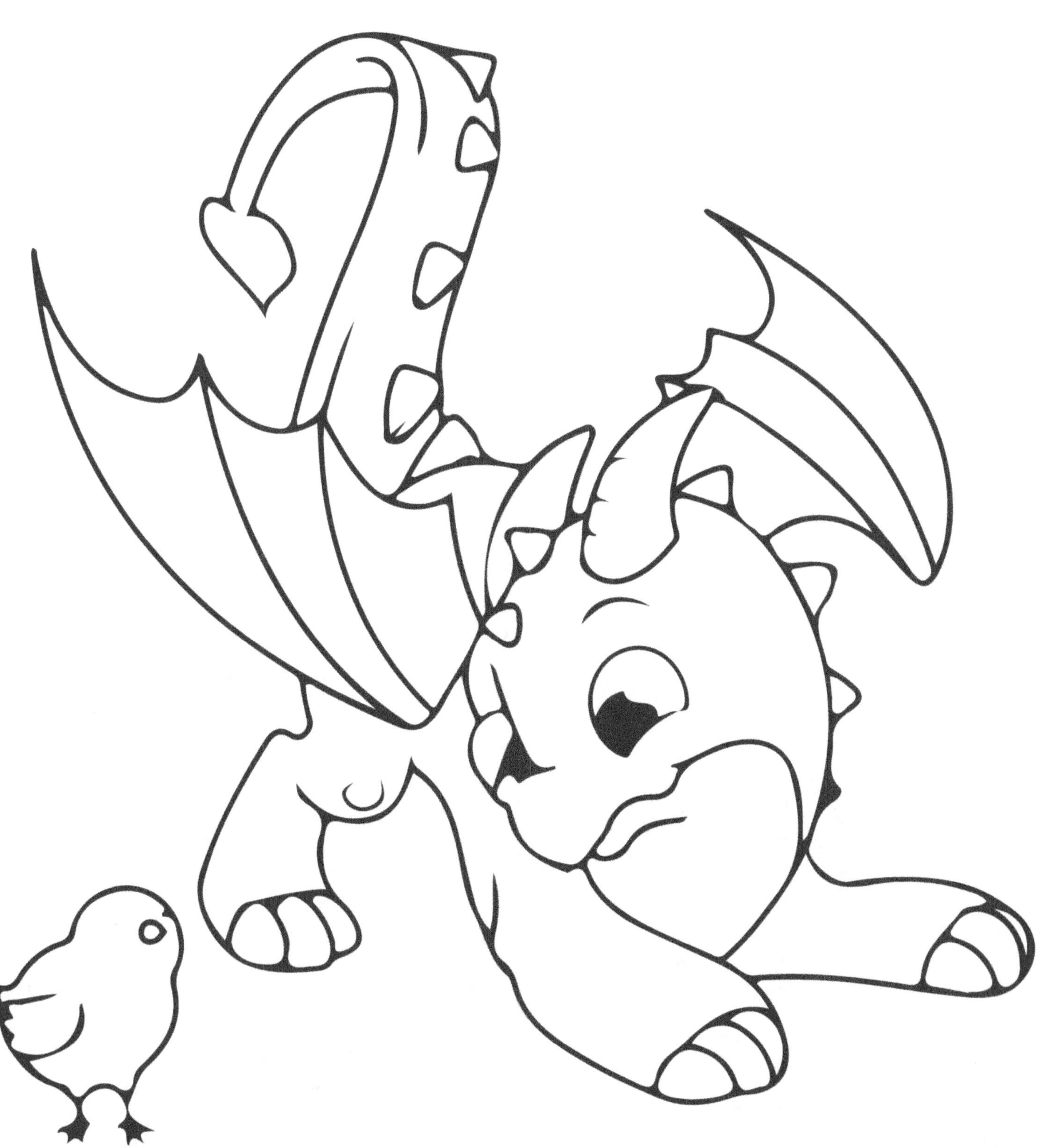

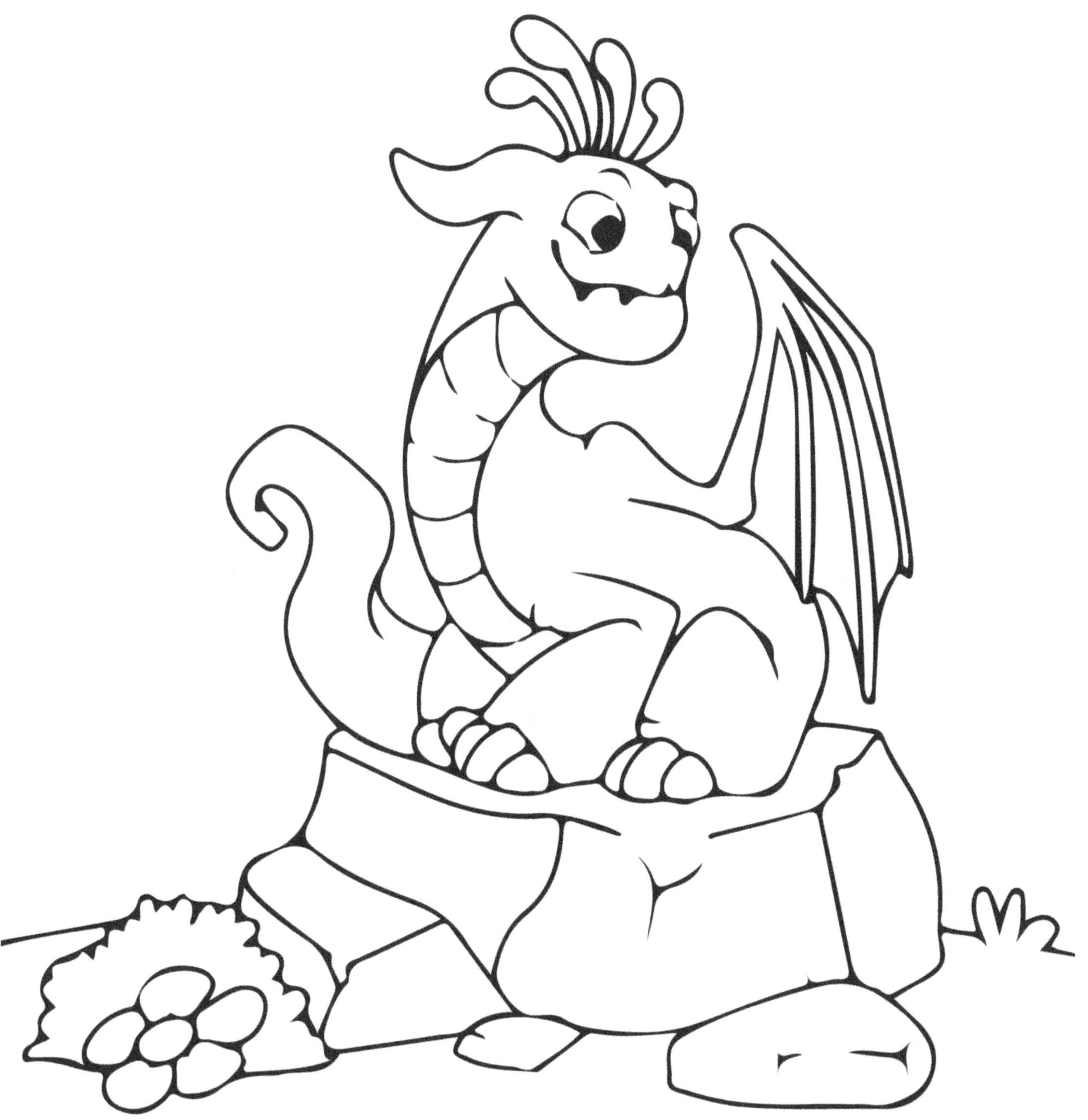

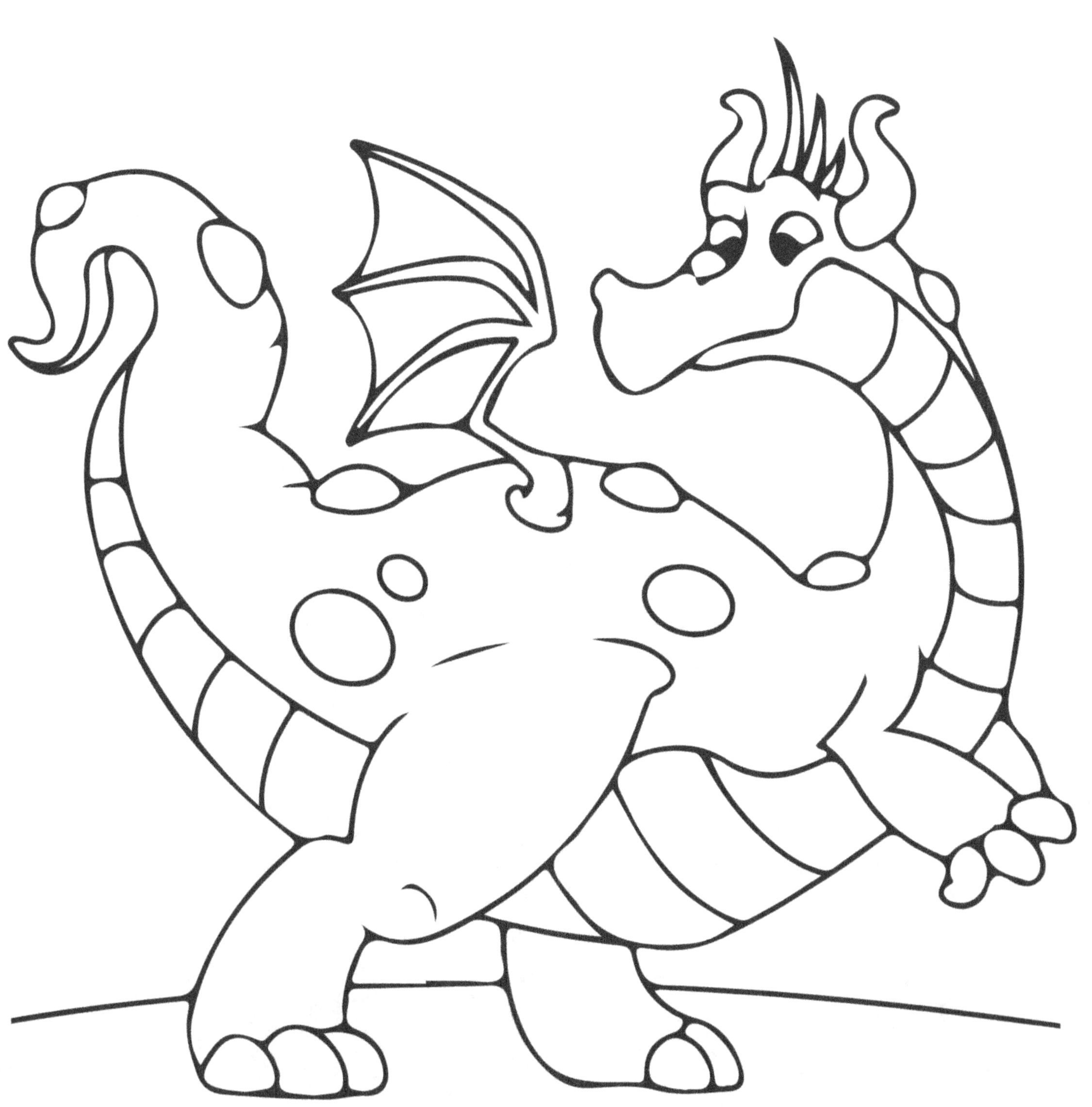

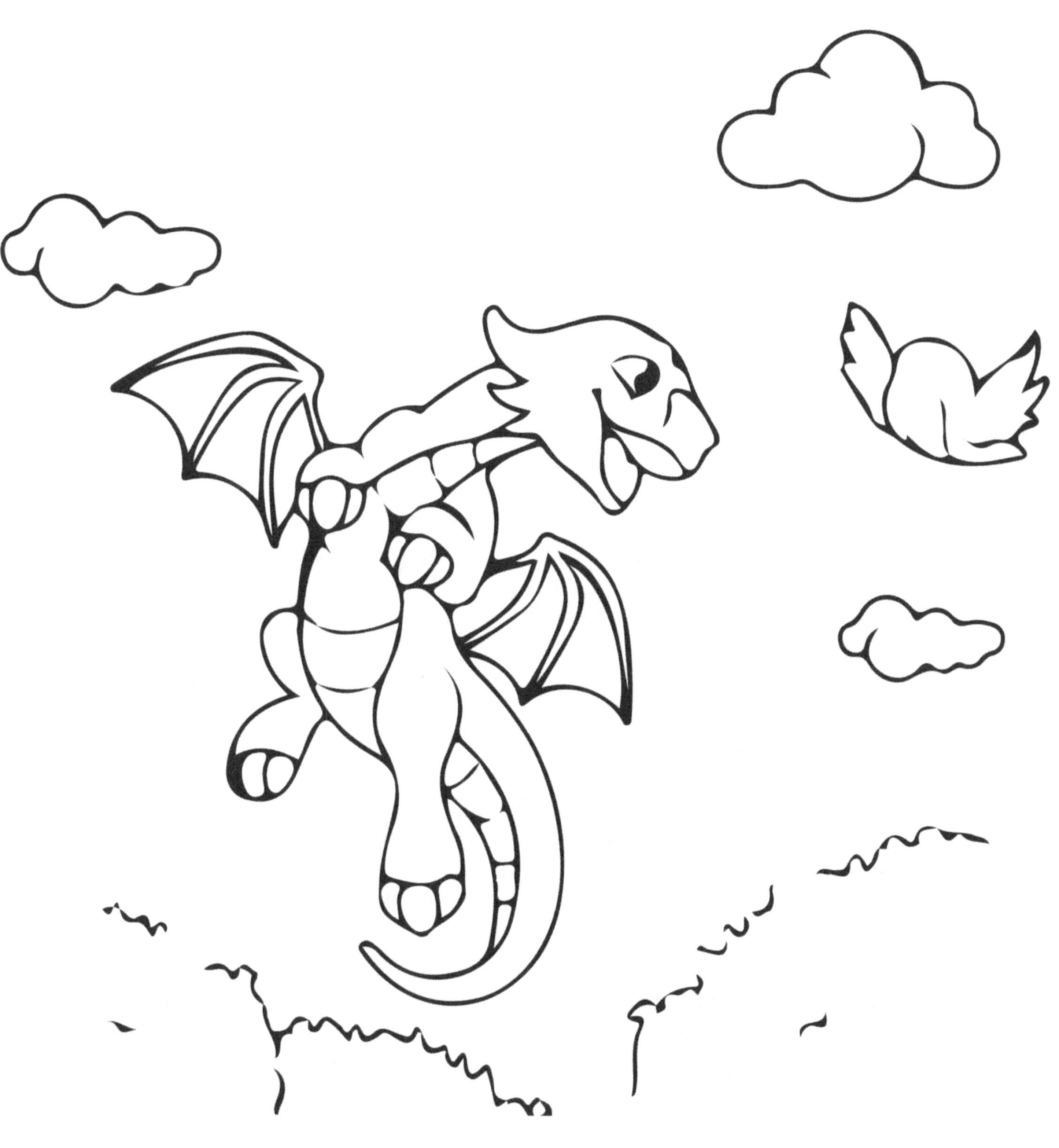

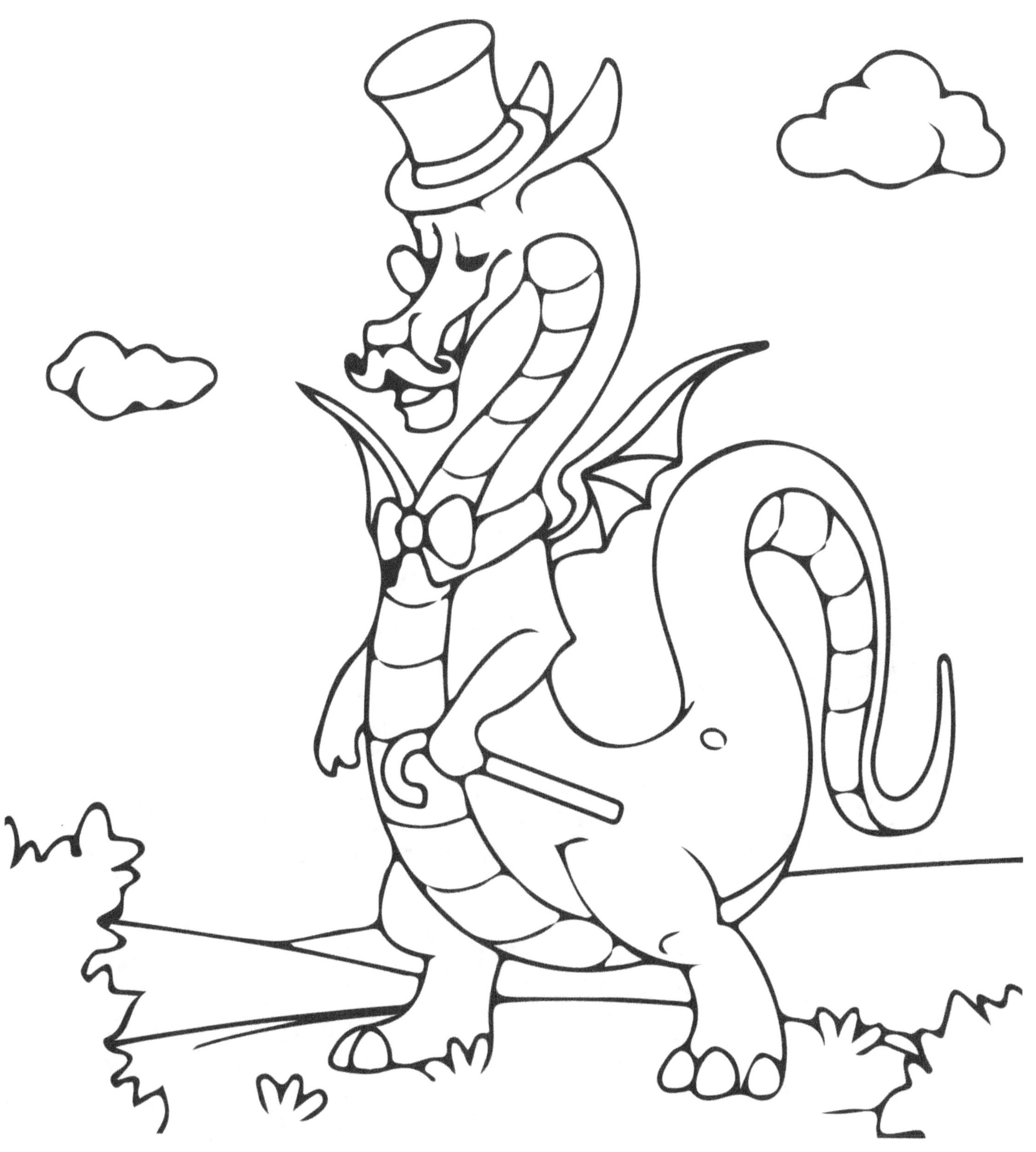

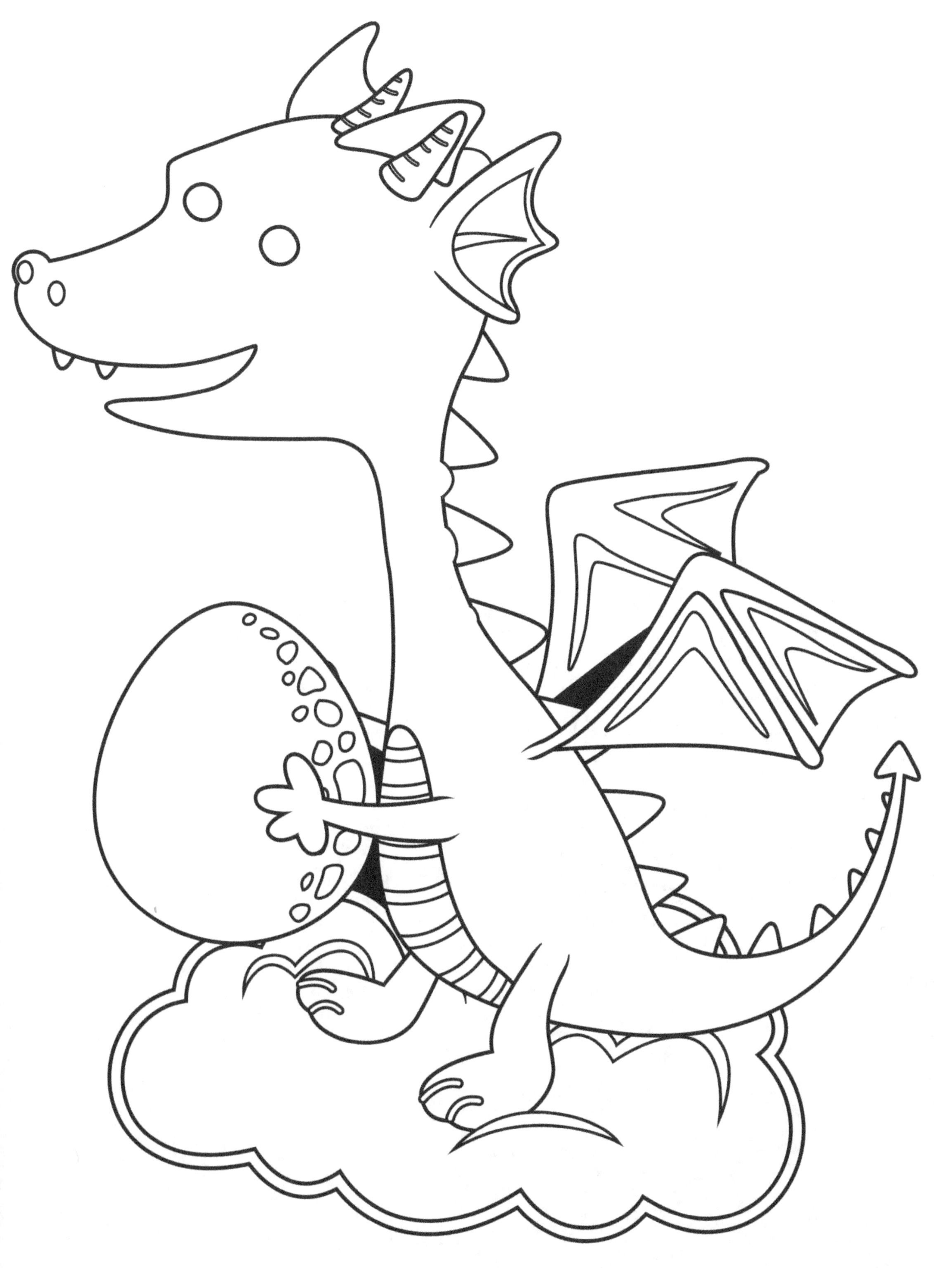

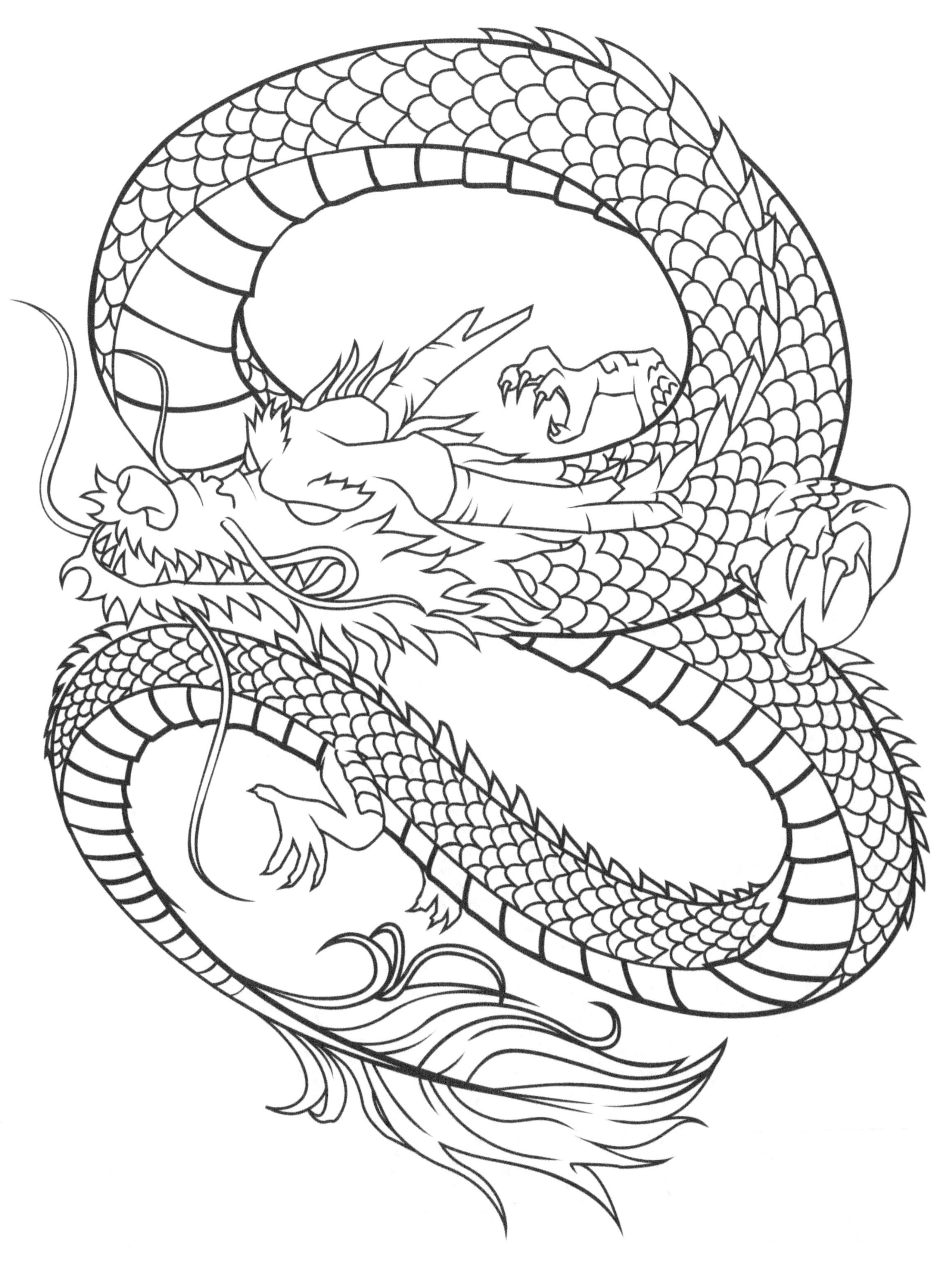

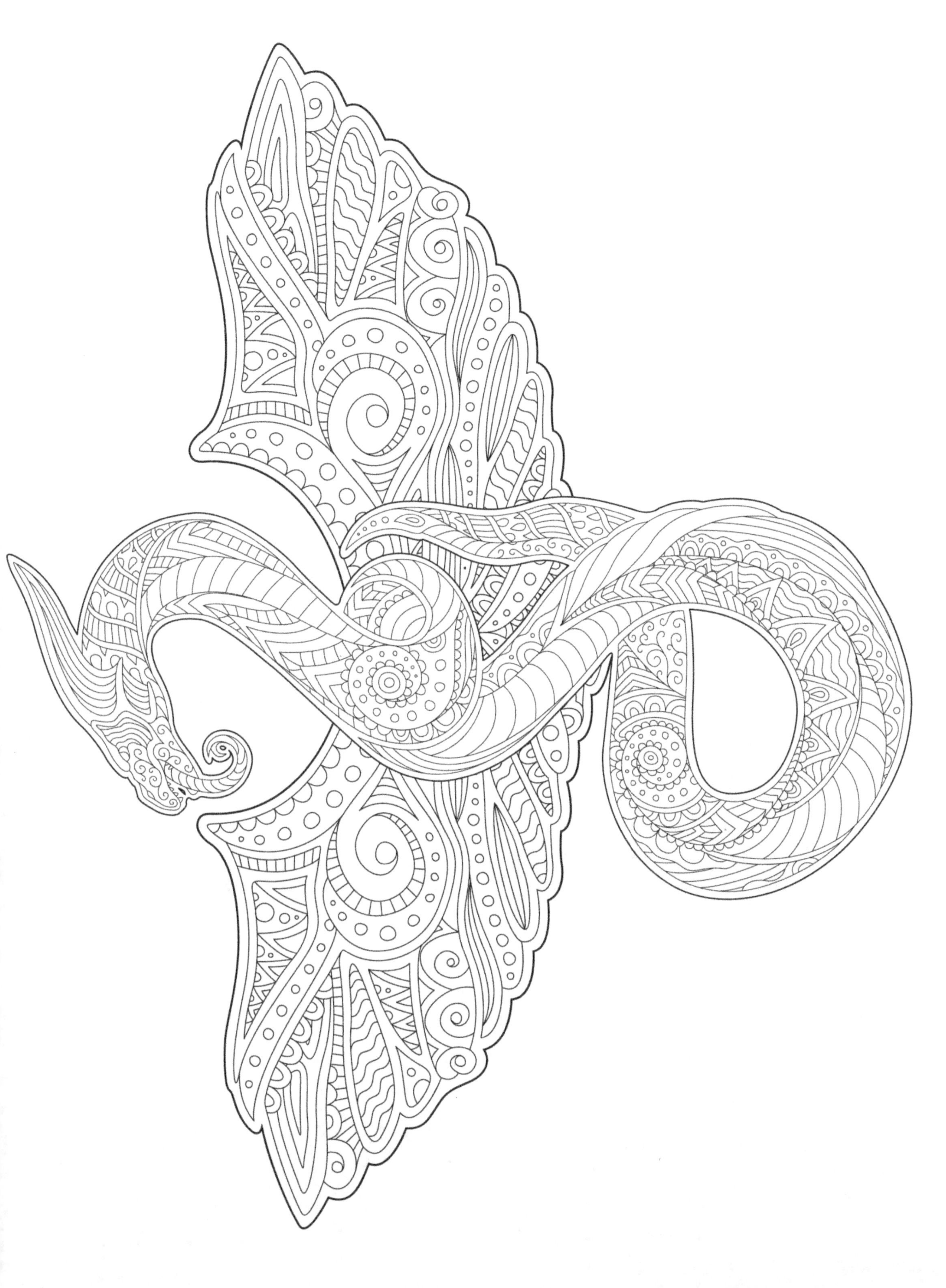

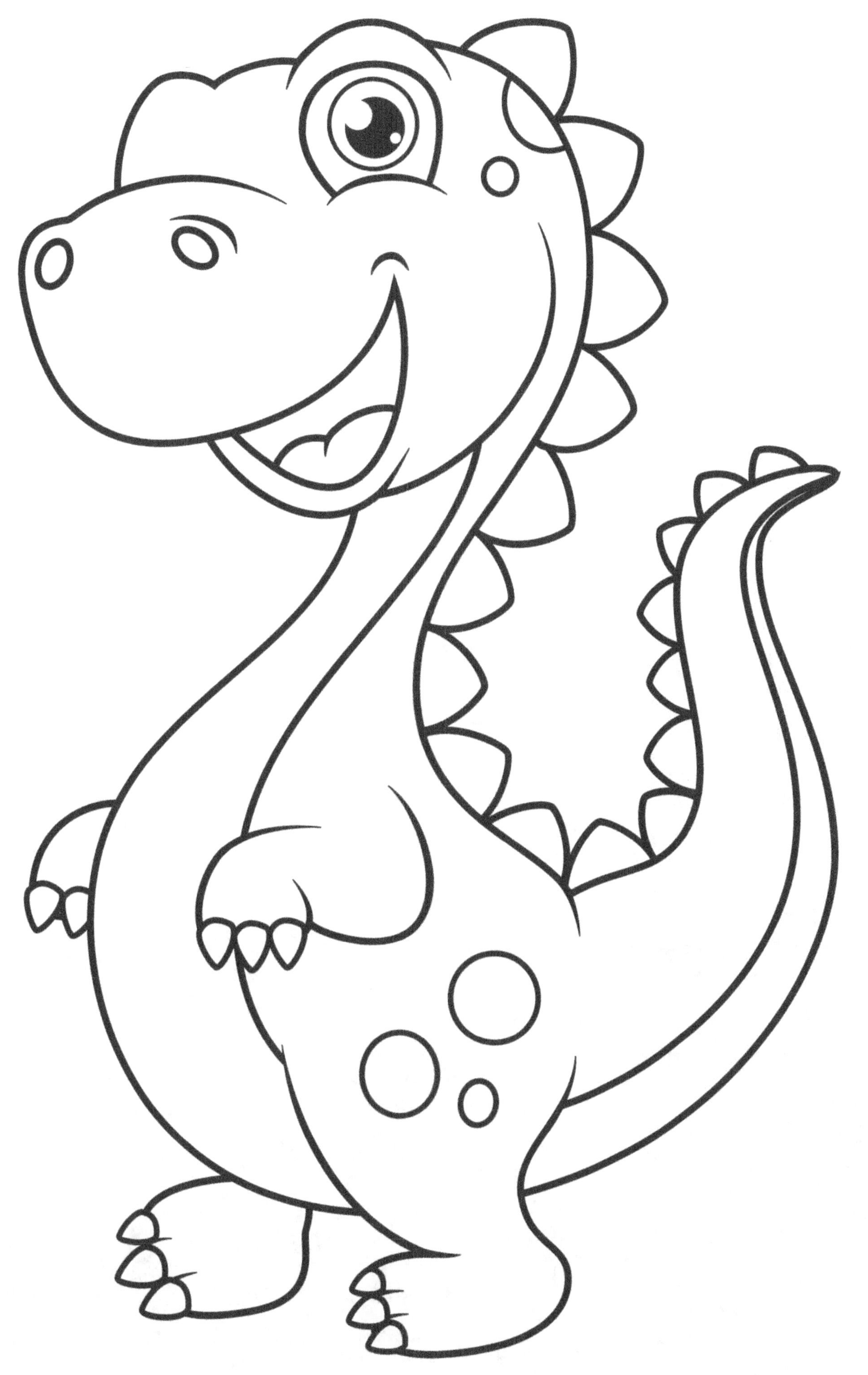

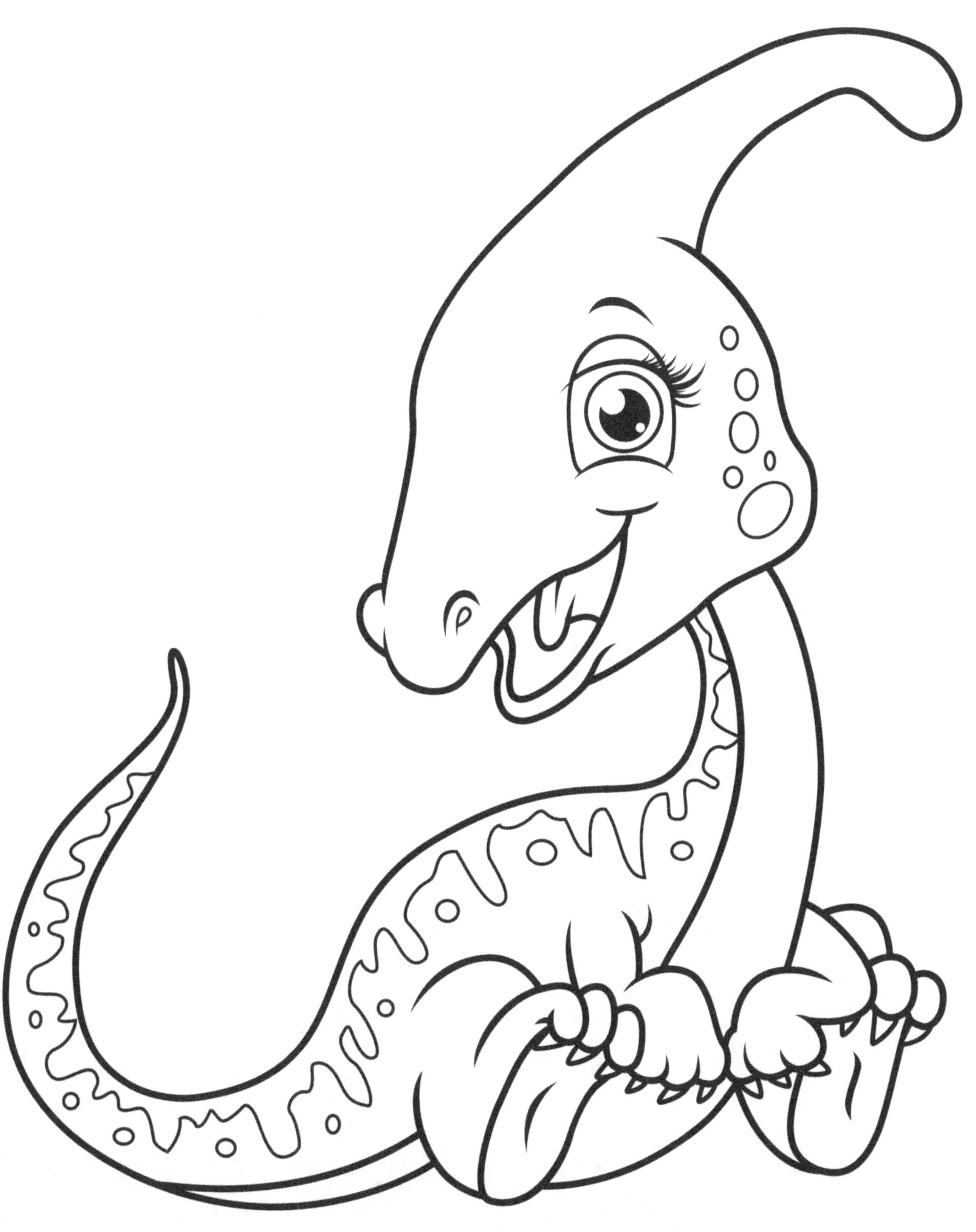

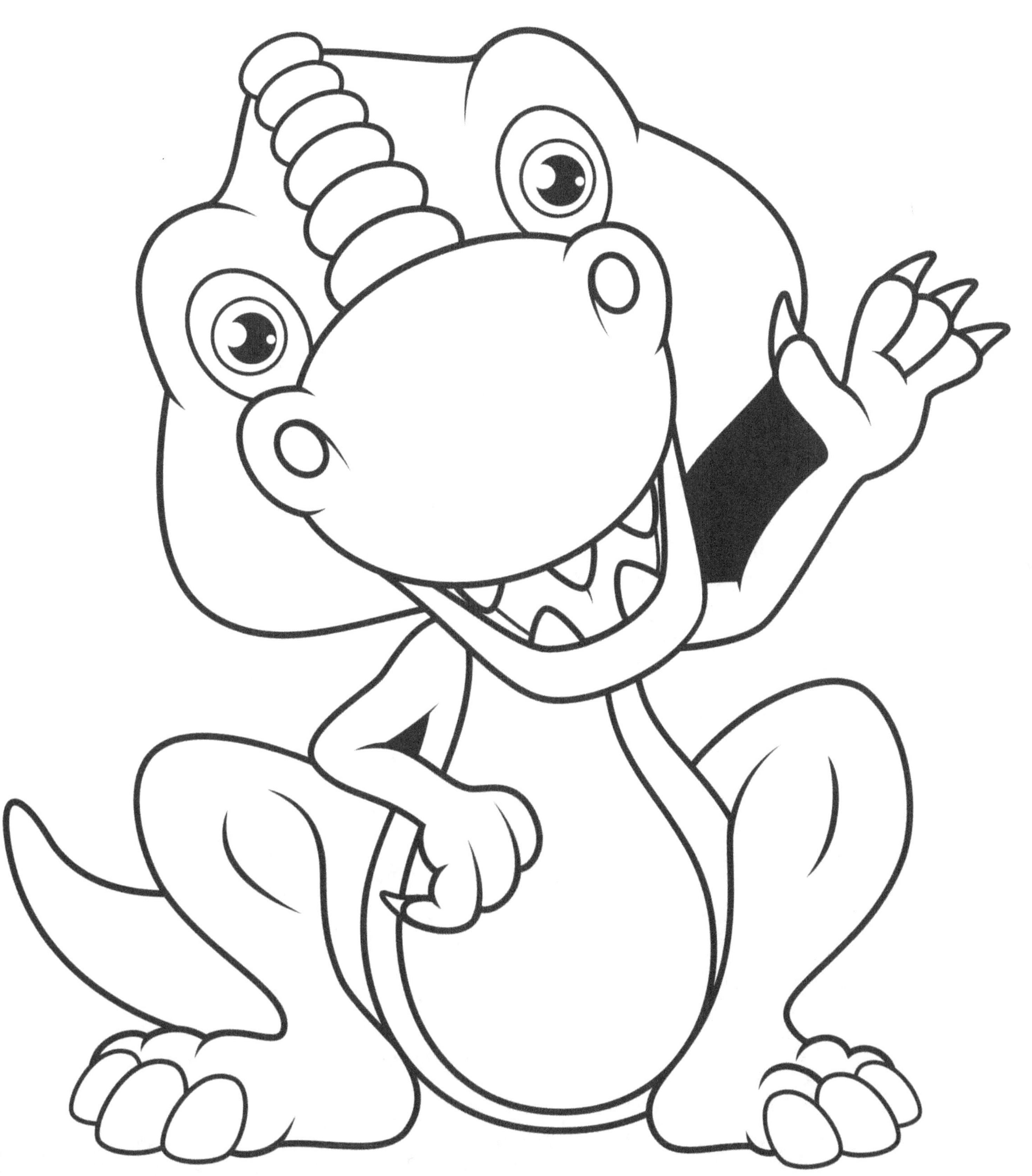

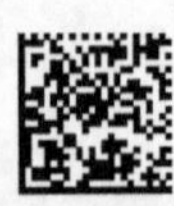

www.ingramcontent.com/pod-product-compliance
Lightning Source LLC
Chambersburg PA
CBHW081430250726

48654CB00013B/1901